Strength for the Body & Soul

Strength for the Body & Soul

31 Recipes, Readings & Reflections

By Sharon Merz

Bladensburg, MD

Strength for the Body & Soul: 31 Readings, Recipes & Reflections
© 2020 by Sharon Merz
All rights reserved.

Unless otherwise indicated, all Scriptures in this book are quoted from The Holy Bible, New International Version ® NIV ®. Copyright © 1973, 1978, 1984, 2011 by Biblica, Inc. ™. Used by permission. All rights reserved worldwide.

Scripture quotations marked MSG are taken from *THE MESSAGE*, copyright © 1993, 2002, 2018 by Eugene H. Peterson. Used by permission of NavPress. All rights reserved. Represented by Tyndale House Publishers, a Division of Tyndale House Ministries.

Scripture quotations marked (NLT) are taken from the Holy Bible, New Living Translation, copyright © 1996, 2004, 2015 by Tyndale House Foundation. Used by permission of Tyndale House Publishers, a Division of Tyndale House Ministries, Carol Stream, Illinois 60188. All rights reserved.

Library of Congress Control Number: 2020949161.

ISBN: 978-1-7359529-2-5

Printed in the United States of America.

All photos by Vicky Pannella.
Design by Anita Leppert and Vicky Pannella.

DEDICATION

This book is dedicated to my best friend, Valerie Gaddis, who in 2007 suggested I start writing devotions based on Scripture. She rarely "appears" in individual devotions, but her constant prayers, support, and encouragement are woven into each line that is written. I am just one of the people whose life has been touched by this incredible woman, who constantly models a servant attitude. Valerie's heart of compassion and unconditional love has inspired me many times to turn to God's word to develop strength for my body and soul. Love you, Sis.

> *"Nehemiah said, 'Go and enjoy choice food and sweet drinks, and send some to those who have nothing prepared. This day is holy to our Lord. Do not grieve, for the joy of the Lord is your strength.'"*
> Nehemiah 8:10

CONTENTS

Introduction
Breakfast Recipes

- #1 Granola Bars
- #2 Cinnamon Donut Muffins
- #3 Breakfast Casserole

Soup & Salad Recipes

- #4 10-Minute Tomato Soup
- #5 Taco Soup
- #6 Sausage Potato Soup
- #7 Sour Cream Potato Salad
- #8 Mexican Garden Salad
- #9 Most Delicious Fruit Salad

Side Dish Recipes

- #10 Cozy Broccoli Casserole
- #11 Spanish Peas
- #12 Sunshine Carrots
- #13 Parmesan Potatoes
- #14 Sunday Rice Casserole
- #15 Dressing/Stuffing
- #16 Creamy Pasta-Veggie Medley
- #17 Secret Sauce for Vegetables

Entrée Recipes

#18 Tamale Pie
#19 Ravioli Casserole
#20 Grilled Salsa Chops
#21 President's Chicken
#22 Chicken 49'ers
#23 Barry's Shrimp Creole
#24 Zippy Baked Fish
#25 Herbed Salmon & Asparagus

Dessert Recipes

#26 Sugar Cookies
#27 Persimmon Cookies
#28 Creamy Pudding Dessert
#29 Apple Pie
#30 Paradise Pumpkin Pie
#31 Fudge Brownie Pie

Author's Notes & Acknowledgments

INTRODUCTION

Who knew that the inspiration for a book could come while cooking dinner? Apparently, God did.

It was my first time preparing Tamale Pie (recipe #18). As the ingredients started to come together, I couldn't help but notice how pretty and colorful the dish was becoming. As a fan of cooking shows, I hear often that "we eat with our eyes first," so I was optimistic that this new dish was a winner on that front. But then I thought about Eve and how she was tempted in the Garden of Eden because that fruit looked really tasty. (That's just how my mind works!) It was at that point that I was inspired to take two of my passions – everyday cooking and my devotions which often just reflect everyday life – and (gulp!) write my first book. It made so much sense as the Tamale Pie made its way into the baking dish. (For the record, it tastes as good as it looks!)

The recipe selection runs the gamut in terms of origin. A couple of them have been traditions in my family since I was a child, while some are recently-discovered gems. Several have been gleaned from community cookbooks, while others have been previously published and I'm grateful for the permissions to use those. I don't even remember where some of the recipes came from, and several of them have been tweaked multiple times to suit my style of cooking, which I refer to as "whatever I feel like making at the time!" No matter the source, I have personally enjoyed each of these recipes and am so delighted to be able to share them.

The greater joy comes in directing others to not only read the Bible, but also to reflect on how it applies to everyday life. Pull up a chair and sample how Joshua is connected to potato salad and James relates to roasted potatoes. It may be hard to imagine how Haggai is linked to a salmon and asparagus dish or Jeremiah to apple pie. But God's word has a lot to say about a lot of things that touch our everyday lives. As busy as life can be, time spent in God's word gives us the strength we need each day, and it can open our mind to the Lord showing us "great and unsearchable things that [we] do not know" (Jeremiah 33:3).

Ready? Let's dig in, and enjoy!

1 Granola Bars

2 cups quick-cooking oats
1 cup all-purpose flour
¾ cup brown sugar
½ cup wheat germ
¾ cup dried fruit (raisins, cranberries, apples, etc.)
½ teaspoon salt
½ teaspoon ground cinnamon
½ cup chopped nuts
½ cup vegetable oil
½ cup honey (a lighter honey is especially good!)
1 egg
4 ounces applesauce
2 teaspoons vanilla extract

Preheat oven to 350°. Line a 9x13 pan with aluminum foil or parchment paper, then coat with cooking spray. In large bowl, stir together the oats, flour, brown sugar, wheat germ, dried fruit, salt, cinnamon, and nuts. In a small bowl, whisk together the oil, honey, egg, applesauce, and vanilla until well blended. Pour over dry ingredients and mix well until the liquid is evenly distributed. Press mixture evenly into prepared pan, wetting hands if necessary. Bake for 20-25 minutes just until the edges are golden. WATCH CAREFULLY: It is <u>very</u> easy to overcook these, which makes them tougher. Cool completely in pan, then turn out onto a cutting board. Remove foil or paper and cut into 12 bars. For best storage, wrap individually and keep in refrigerator or freezer.

Reading: Luke 10:38-42

I had a situation with a friend of mine who was battling cancer. He had written me with some information, and then shortly afterwards posted some information in a web journal that to me seemed contradictory. The journal entry indicated how difficult the treatments were, while he had indicated to me he was doing very well. I was puzzled, because this friend isn't the type to contradict himself. Before I questioned him about it, however, I decided to check with another friend -- a cancer survivor who has also met the first friend.

The second friend said he didn't think the information was contradictory and gave me an explanation that made perfect sense. He put things into perspective: he said the blog was just general information, but he would have been in a better mood having heard from a friend, which is why his response to me was more upbeat.

Most people consider breakfast to be the most important meal of the day. A nutritious beginning like Granola Bars can set the pace for the coming day. Another great way to start the day is having a quiet time with God that starts with reading Scriptures. What is your perspective when you read the Bible? Do you view it as a "general" posting, or do you approach it with a positive mood because you're hearing from a friend?

God has always desired an intimate relationship with His creation. Genesis 3 talks about God "walking in the garden in the cool of the day," and Exodus 33:11 tells us, "The Lord would speak to Moses face to face, as a man speaks with his friend." Jesus walked among men to fellowship with them and show His friendship before giving His life for the world. Jesus talked to His disciples about friendship in John 15, stating in verse 15, "I have called you friends, for everything that I learned from the Father I have made known to you." In Luke 10 we see a young woman named Mary set aside some pressing priorities because of her intense desire to hear from Jesus.

Approach your time reading the Bible and praying with a different perspective -- expect to hear from a friend!

Cinnamon Donut Muffins

3 ½ cups flour
3 teaspoons baking powder
1 teaspoon each salt & ground nutmeg
½ teaspoon ground cinnamon
1 ½ cup sugar
2/3 cup vegetable oil
2 eggs, lightly beaten
1 ½ cup milk
½ cup applesauce
TOPPING:
4 tablespoons butter
2/3 cup sugar
2 teaspoons cinnamon

Combine flour, baking powder, salt, nutmeg and cinnamon in a large bowl. (I like to replace those spices with 1 tablespoon Madison Baking Spice from Galena Garlic Co. in Madison, IN for an even better flavor!) Combine sugar, oil, eggs & milk; stir into dry ingredients with applesauce just until moistened. Fill paper-lined muffin cups ¾ full with the batter. Bake at 350° for 20-25 minutes or until done. Place melted butter in a small bowl; combine sugar & cinnamon in another bowl. After removing muffins from oven, dip tops in butter, then in cinnamon-sugar mixture. Makes about 20 muffins.

Reading: 2 Corinthians 2:14-17

One time I was shopping with someone whose eyes were drawn to a certain pin. Although not one to wear pins, this person felt compelled to purchase this particular item. It wasn't fancy: it was just a small, green square with these words in black type: "There's that smell again." It was the amusing phrase that inspired the uncharacteristic purchase.

Oddly enough, the Bible seems to endorse that phrase, implying we all give off a "smell". Cinnamon Donut Muffins create an incredible smell as they're baking, but the Bible is referring to something different. The apostle Paul, who enjoyed making analogies, mentions this aroma that we all emit. The way Paul puts it, how we smell to others depends on the perspective of their noses. In 2 Corinthians 2:15-16, he explains that Christians are "the aroma of Christ among those who are being saved and those who are perishing. To the one we are the smell of death; to the other, the fragrance of life."

Just think: to everyone you meet you smell like either life or death. It's certainly something to think about. And Paul ends verse 16 with a fitting and thought-provoking question: "And who is equal to such a task?" We all know that smells have varying degrees of strength and our individual "essence of Christianity" is no different. A non-believer around me may sniff and detect a slight odor of death because I don't use or condone crude language, but they'd get a big whiff of death if I'd actually share the gospel with them! Fellow believers might catch a faint smell of life wafting from me as I smile and ask how they are, but they might be knocked over with an overpowering fragrance of life if I would ask how I could be praying for them or would minister to them in a personal, specific way.

If you think our odors don't rise any higher than our noses, think again. The apostle John tells us in Revelation 5:8 that in heaven he saw "golden bowls full of incense, which are the prayers of God's people." How has your potpourri of prayer been lately? A pleasing smell tends to lighten our steps, so just think how much joy God must receive as He inhales the fragrant prayer offerings of his people! Hard as it may be to imagine, it's even more enjoyable than the smell of Cinnamon Donut Muffins baking!

So if you think you can't identify with "there's that smell again," maybe you'd better give a sniff -- and make sure your odor is Christlike.

Breakfast Casserole

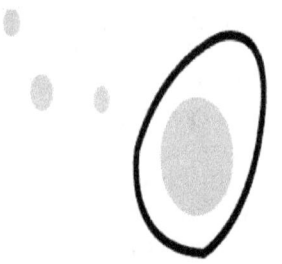

1 pound bulk sausage, browned & cooled slightly
6 eggs, beaten
1 cup shredded cheddar cheese
2 cups milk
1 teaspoon salt
1 teaspoon dry mustard
6 slices bread, finely crumbled

Add beaten eggs to sausage, then combine remainder of ingredients. Mix all together & put in greased 9" x 13" pan. Refrigerate overnight. Bake in 350° oven for 45 minutes.

Reading: Isaiah 40:1-5

One time I attended a college senior's piano recital. He played classical music beautifully for more than an hour without a single sheet in front of him. He drew a nice-sized audience and we all knew that this talented young man had truly spent years preparing for this special night!

That same year I was really "getting into" the Advent season more than I previously had. I haven't always attended churches that put a lot of focus on Advent, but the church I attended at that time was putting an extra focus on it. In addition to the weekly lighting of Advent candles and listening to the corresponding readings, I personally was reading two Advent devotionals and had attended a Service of Lessons and Carols for the first time (which I highly recommend). Advent has to do with preparing for Christmas – for celebrating the day Jesus was born. I once heard someone say, "Life is Advent; life is recognizing the coming of the Lord."

It makes sense to "be prepared" as the Scout motto declares. We should prepare for some of life's smaller tasks, like a school assignment or preparing to cook a dish. One example is this Breakfast Casserole, which is actually prepared the night before baking. We always prepare for the big things in our lives – piano recitals, graduations, going to college, weddings, and the birth of babies. Preparing for the birth of the Holy Child should be no less important. Preparation makes us plan ahead. It makes us think carefully about what is about to happen and the impact it will have on our lives.

God Himself knew the world needed to prepare for the arrival of Jesus. In comforting God's people, the prophet Isaiah wrote: "A voice of one calling: 'In the desert prepare the way for the Lord; make straight in the wilderness a highway for our God...'" (Isaiah 40:3) The Message translation says: "Prepare for God's arrival!" This was a prophecy about John the Baptist, and he knew his role in God's plan. Matthew 3:11 records his words: "I baptize you with water for repentance. But after me will come one who is more powerful than I, whose sandals I am not fit to carry. He will baptize you with the Holy Spirit and with fire." John the Baptist had prepared himself, and fulfilled his role of helping others get ready for Christ's coming.

Get ready – Christmas is coming, no matter what time of year it actually is! It is a wonderful time to celebrate, for it is at that time that we focus on Emmanuel, which means "God with us." Can you think of a more blessed event? I can't. Be prepared!

10-Minute Tomato Soup

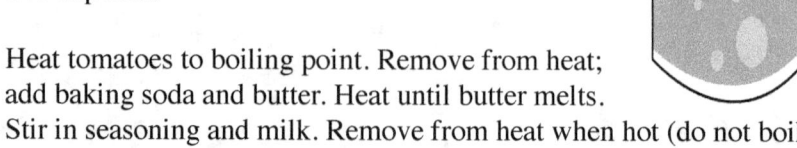

29-ounce can crushed tomatoes
½ teaspoon baking soda
2 tablespoons butter
Garlic powder & basil to taste
1 ½ cup milk

Heat tomatoes to boiling point. Remove from heat; add baking soda and butter. Heat until butter melts. Stir in seasoning and milk. Remove from heat when hot (do not boil).

Reading: Psalm 74:12-17

Asaph pens of the Lord in Psalm 74:17, "It was you who set all the boundaries of the earth; you made both summer and winter."

We need boundaries. We don't like boundaries, though. We feel they are too limiting, too restrictive. Yes, we don't like boundaries, but we need them. Just as parents set boundaries for their children for their own protection, God sets boundaries for us.

But even though we tend to consider boundaries to be limiting, God creates them for us not just for our protection, but also for our growth.

If that doesn't make sense to you, think about tomato cages. I am not personally a gardener, but I've been around enough of them to understand the purpose of tomato cages. Tomato plants are almost always spindly at the onset. They struggle to grow tall on their own, so gardeners support them with wire cages. The cages provide protection from some animals, but also give the tomato plants direction which actually aids growth. This is how a tomato plant grows strong and healthy. Without well-grown tomatoes, it wouldn't be easy to make a lot of great-tasting dishes, like 10-Minute Tomato Soup.

Christians are like tomato plants. We start off a little shaky and uncertain of our own strength, as well as our ability to bear fruit. But God in His loving care places us in the tomato cages known as churches, which provide protection and direction so we can grow stronger. There are also many "varieties" of Christians who will bear different fruits, just as there are numerous tomato varieties. But each has its own merits, and God loves and tends each one to allow us to provide a bumper crop of blessings to others!

Taco Soup

1 pound hamburger, browned & drained
1 package taco seasoning
1 package ranch dressing mix
29-ounce can diced tomatoes
15-ounce can creamed corn
15-ounce can kidney beans

Combine all ingredients in Dutch oven (don't drain canned items), adding water to desired consistency. Heat through.

Reading: 1 Kings 8:10-14

Those who know me can vouch for the fact that I just enjoy food. I like the creative process of cooking, but I also enjoy eating. There's just something about good food that is so satisfying, and I think that's something most everyone can identify with.

Sometimes, the food being served is so good, however, that we eat too much. Especially in the winter, a steaming bowl of tasty, homemade soup like Taco Soup is just unbeatable to me so it's hard to stop going back for more! Rare is the person who has never said, "I ate so much that I couldn't put another bite in my mouth." Getting full is not usually the goal of eating a meal, but is oftentimes the outcome!

Being full of too much food can be uncomfortable, but fullness is not always a bad thing. A full tank of gas is something that gives great security. But the Bible talks about the greatest sense of fullness there is. 1 Kings 8:11b reads in The Message: "The glory of God filled The Temple of God!" In the context, the writer was describing how the priests couldn't perform their duties in the newly-built temple because it was filled with a cloud -- the presence of God.

While that's an Old Testament reference about a building in Jerusalem, it is very relevant to us today. Paul writes in 1 Corinthians 3:16: "You realize, don't you, that you are the temple of God, and God himself is present in you?" (MSG) Later in that same book, he tells Christians, "Do you not know that your body is a temple of the Holy Spirit, who is in you, whom you have received from God? You are not your own." (1 Corinthians 6:19, NIV) Paul brings up the subject again in 2 Corinthians 6:16, when he says, "For we are the temple of the living God."

The Bible is pretty clear -- Christians are God's temple. How amazing it would be if we would all allow ourselves to be totally filled by God! It would be incredible if people could see our Heavenly Father so plainly in control of our lives that they would say of us, "The glory of God filled The Temple of God!" Getting full of God's glory is far more satisfying than any meal could ever be!

Sausage Potato Soup

3 large potatoes, peeled & cubed
1-2 cloves garlic, minced or crushed
2 cups milk
1 stick butter
1 cup broccoli, chopped
1 onion, diced or chopped
½ cup celery, diced
Ground black pepper, cayenne pepper, & salt to taste
½ teaspoon Louisiana hot sauce (or to taste)
1 package brown & serve sausage links

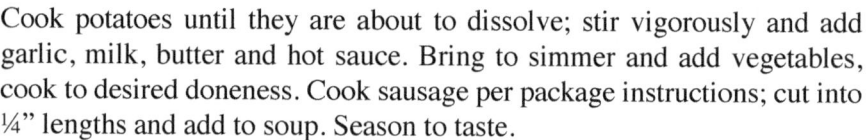

Cook potatoes until they are about to dissolve; stir vigorously and add garlic, milk, butter and hot sauce. Bring to simmer and add vegetables, cook to desired doneness. Cook sausage per package instructions; cut into ¼" lengths and add to soup. Season to taste.

Used by permission of Rex K. Brown, who likes this soup very spicy!

Reading: Romans 12:3-8

I was down -- way, way down. And I had been there for several days. A friend – the same one who came up with this soup recipe – dropped by my house to help me with something and could tell something was wrong and became quite concerned. Later, as I decided to open up, I revealed how empty and futile I felt my life was because I wasn't doing great big things for God's kingdom. He then began to tell me about all the people we knew together who thought a lot about me.

Reminding me that all Christians have an impact on the kingdom of God in our own ways, he attempted to show me that I was no different. "You have no idea what the little things you have done for me and for others means. You're a sweet soul and a good friend, and we have all been enriched by your presence." Sensing I still wasn't seeing it, he added, "I wish I had a magic mirror to put in your face that showed what others see in you."

My friend admitted that is a common problem -- we all have a tough time seeing how we touch the lives around us. That's why I think it's so important that we all do what this friend did for me -- share with people in our lives what they mean to us. In this dog-eat-dog world, encouragement is rare so it is like gold when it is sincere.

Encouragement is also biblical -- in fact, Romans 12:8 mentions it as a spiritual gift. Paul writes in 1 Thessalonians 4:18, "Therefore encourage each other." The writer of Hebrews also made a point of saying "But encourage one another daily, as long as it is called 'Today,' so that none of you may be hardened by sin's deceitfulness" (3:13).

Many people refer to their daily allotment of coffee as a "cup of courage." Perhaps we should make a habit of sharing a "cup of encourage." That week, my cup was low -- it may have even been completely empty from lack of encouragement. I'm thankful for friends who brew up the right words to lift my spirits when I need them. Don't let the cups of those around you run dry. Be that "magic mirror" to show how others see them. And as you encourage others, you will be blessed and can join David as he declares in Psalm 23:5, "my cup overflows"!

Sour Cream Potato Salad

5 pounds potatoes; peeled, cubed and cooked
1 cup diced celery
16 ounces sour cream
4 eggs
2 tablespoons apple cider vinegar
1 teaspoon salt
1 teaspoon ground pepper
3 tablespoons mustard
1 clove garlic, minced
1 small onion or 2 large green onions, chopped

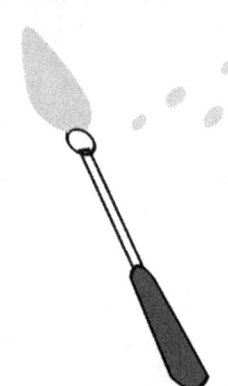

Chill potatoes. Add celery; toss lightly. Place sour cream in small mixing bowl. In small saucepan, cover eggs with water and cook just until boiling point (you aren't hard boiling these, just coddling them; even the whites should still be slightly runny). Remove from heat; spoon into sour cream. Mix well. Add remaining ingredients; mix well. Add dressing to potatoes and stir to coat. Chill for at least 3 hours before serving.

Reading: Joshua 22:1-5

It was 7:30 a.m. on a weekday morning. I was almost done peeling the 5-pound bag of potatoes that I needed for the batch of Sour Cream Potato Salad that was going to help feed 18 people -- mostly teen-agers -- at lunch later that day. The starch from the spuds was all over my hands and I could tell it would be easy for one of the potatoes to take flight. Since I was in my living room where I could enjoy the breeze from the ceiling fan, I started to worry if a potato projectile would damage a lamp, the television, computer, etc. Fortunately, no appliances were harmed in the making of the potato salad!

It made me think, though, how difficult some things can be to hold onto. The potatoes -- once you've peeled one end and the center, leaving only the other end to be peeled -- can get quite slick. Some things aren't even worth holding onto. So what is?

As with everything, the Bible has the answer! Here's just a sampling:

"Let us hold unswervingly to the hope we profess, for he who promised is faithful" (Hebrews 10:23).

"But test everything that is said. Hold on to what is good" (1 Thessalonians 5:21, NLT).

"They must keep hold of the deep truths of the faith with a clear conscience" (1 Timothy 3:9).

"He must hold firmly to the trustworthy message as it has been taught, so that he can encourage others by sound doctrine and refute those who oppose it" (Titus 1:9).

"But be very careful to keep the commandment and the law that Moses the servant of the Lord gave you: to love the Lord your God, to walk in obedience to him, to keep his commands, to hold fast to him and to serve him with all your heart and with all your soul" (Joshua 22:5).

What are you holding onto?

Mexican Garden Salad

1 medium tomato, chopped (about 1 cup)
1 cup diced cucumber
1 cup chopped sweet onion
1 medium avocado, peeled and chopped
½ cup chopped fresh cilantro
1 tablespoon lime juice
¼ teaspoon ground cumin
¼ teaspoon salt (optional)
1/8 teaspoon ground black pepper.

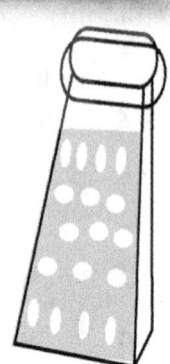

In medium bowl, mix vegetables with remaining ingredients. Serve as is or on a bed of lettuce.

Used with permission. Brenda J. Ponichtera, Quick & Healthy Recipes and Ideas, 3rd edition, Arlington, VA., Small Steps Press (American Diabetes Association), 342 pages, 2013.

Reading: Matthew 26:36-44

I have a brown thumb. I've come to terms with this over the years, especially since being a botanist was a pre-teen aspiration. My parents tried to encourage this by letting me pick out a package of seeds to plant. However, my pot of bachelor buttons pretty much stayed a pot of dirt. Over the years I have successfully killed many a houseplant although at one point I had a planter that miraculously survived a few months under my care.

Plants are wonderful and lush, ornate gardens with wide varieties of trees, flowers and foliage seem to draw people to them with their beauty, but also with their atmosphere of serenity. This is how I picture the Garden of Gethsemane, where Jesus spent a lot of time in prayer just prior to His crucifixion and the ultimate resurrection which we celebrate on Easter each year. I am drawn to this garden because it is where I feel closest to Jesus.

As you read the accounts of Jesus in that garden in the first three gospels (Matthew 26:36-46, Mark 14:32-42 and Luke 22:39-46) you get to see just how human Jesus was during His time on earth. Jesus tells His disciples, "My soul is overwhelmed with sorrow to the point of death" (Matthew 26:38) as He was "deeply distressed and troubled" (Mark 14:33). Three times He prayed "take this cup from me" -- Jesus did not want to die. When He came back and found Peter, James and John unable to stay awake He became a little frustrated with them -- He wanted the support of His closest friends during His time of distress. Jesus agonized over what He had been called to do so much so that Luke records "And being in anguish, he prayed more earnestly, and his sweat was like drops of blood falling to the ground" (Luke 22:44).

When we think of a vegetable garden, we think of the harvest -- what we will be taking out of the garden. There are a lot of good things we get to make from that harvest, like the ingredients for a Mexican Garden Salad. Jesus' harvest from the Garden of Gethsemane was a strengthened resolve to obey and do God's will. This harvest took Him to the cross -- our cross -- so that we would have an example.

Are you struggling with doing God's will in any areas? Follow the plan of the Master Gardener: give the matter a generous amount of prayer that you may enjoy a harvest of obedience. Jesus struggled just as we all struggle, yet He knew how to overcome human nature by taking it to God and submitting to Him. Come join the harvest!

Most Delicious Fruit Salad

15 ½-ounce can pineapple tidbits
1 can mandarin oranges
1 ½ cup frozen strawberries
3 bananas, sliced
1 can peach pie filling

Drain canned fruit; add strawberries and bananas. Stir in pie filling and refrigerate. Will keep 2-3 days.

Reading: Psalm 92:12-15

As I get older, I realize what that really means. My body just works a little differently than it used to, from my brain to my back. For a recent birthday, my oldest sister sent me a card that said on the front "Do you want to know what's good about getting old?" Inside it read, "As soon as I find something I'll tell you."

I can increasingly appreciate the humor regarding old age, like these tidbits emailed to me by one of my cousins:

"The older you get, the tougher it is to lose weight, because by then your body and your fat have gotten to be really good friends."

"The older we get, the fewer things seem worth waiting in line for."

"When you are dissatisfied and would like to go back to youth, think of algebra."

And one of my favorites, seemingly filled with sarcasm: "One of the many things no one tells you about aging is that it is such a nice change from being young."

While I chuckle at things like this, I do think about how I want to age. I see some people who not only carry their age like a burden but also make it a point of sharing it with others. Then I see others who choose to carry a smile instead -- and make it a point of sharing it with others. I pray that I will age gracefully like that, aiming to be a blessing rather than a burden to others.

Psalm 92:14 has an even more ambitious take on aging: "They will still bear fruit in old age, they will stay fresh and green." I think it means that serving others has no end. As I get older I might not be able to play softball with the youth as part of my ministry, but maybe I can bake them cookies for the fellowship time afterwards. The verse also implies that if I choose to become a pew potato, I will wilt.

The secret of youth, according to the Bible, is to continue to bear fruit so we can stay fresh and green. People prefer being around those who are "fresh" as opposed to those who are "stale." And when different people in a body of believers bear fruit and combine them, the end result is even more satisfying than the flavors of this great fruit salad.

It always helps to have a fresh perspective on things, like this other thought my cousin sent me: "There's always a lot to be thankful for if you take time to look for it. For example, I am sitting here thinking how nice it is that wrinkles don't hurt."

Side Dishes

Cozy Broccoli Casserole

1 ½ pound fresh broccoli
2 eggs, slightly beaten
¾ cup cottage cheese
½ cup shredded cheddar cheese
2 tablespoons finely chopped onion
½ teaspoon ground pepper
1 teaspoon Worcestershire sauce
¼ cup dry bread crumbs
1 tablespoon melted butter

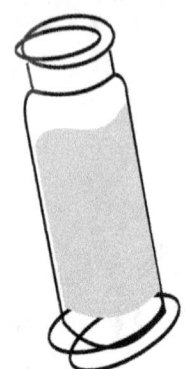

Trim broccoli and cut into spears. Cook in a small amount of water in saucepan for 10 minutes; drain. Place in lightly-greased 1 ½-quart baking dish. Combine eggs, cottage cheese, cheddar cheese, onion, pepper, and Worcestershire sauce in bowl; mix well. Spoon over broccoli. Toss bread crumbs with melted butter; sprinkle over casserole. Bake at 350° for 15-20 minutes or until bubbly.

Reading: 2 Corinthians 1:3-7

I got a call one evening from one of the ladies of the church. The woman asked if I would be interested in providing an item for a funeral dinner scheduled in a couple of days. She still had three things she needed: a corn casserole, gelatin salad or deviled eggs. I told her I had made many a corn casserole over the years, so I'd be happy to supply that.

As we chatted briefly, the woman told me that one time she was calling for items and mentioned green bean casserole. The person she was asking thought that wasn't a very impressive dish to serve at a funeral dinner. The organizer explained that she believed the friends and family would better appreciate an ordinary dish because it signified comfort food. And comfort is really what a funeral dinner is all about, she told me.

The apostle Paul agreed with this woman wholeheartedly. In the first chapter of 2 Corinthians, he offers praise to God "who comforts us in all our troubles, so that we can comfort those in any trouble with the comfort we ourselves have received from God" (verse 4).

Most of us have received some sort of comfort in one situation or another. The body of Christ should be the leader when it comes to giving comfort because of "the Father of compassion and the God of all comfort," as Paul describes Him in verse 3. Comfort is special because it's from the heart of God.

Look around you for those in need of comfort -- I can almost guarantee they won't be hard to find. Then let God show you what type of comfort they need. One person might need a hug; another, an encouraging word. Yet another might just need an ordinary vegetable casserole, whether it contains corn, green beans, or even broccoli.

11   Spanish Peas

1 ½ cup frozen peas, heated and drained
½ cup mayonnaise
½ cup sour cream
2 tablespoons chopped pimento
2 tablespoons chopped onion
2 tablespoons chopped bell pepper
Dash of seasoned salt
2 tablespoons chopped parsley

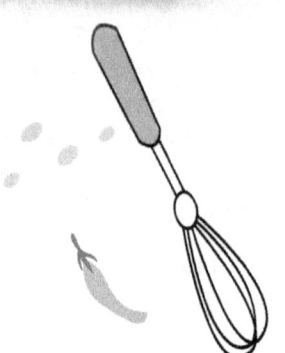

While peas are heating, mix remaining ingredients; pour over drained peas; stir gently to mix.

Note: Sauce can be made ahead of time and will keep several days.

Reading: Philippians 4:4-7

I have to admit that when I hear the word "peace" – and even sometimes when I hear "peas" – I oftentimes think of a line from a Mel Brooks film from a number of years ago. The famous comedian and producer was playing in an underground theater troupe during World War 2, and Brooks was playing the part of Adolf Hitler. As the German dictator, Brooks was explaining that he wasn't an aggressive warmonger when Brooks breaks into song: "All I want is peace! Peace! A little piece of Poland, a little piece of France…"

So you understand that occasionally I have to remind myself that peace is a very serious subject. The news anchors are constantly bombarding us with that word in a variety of forms, so we hear it a lot. As a church, we are often called to pray for peace when certain violent situations arise in various parts of the world. But what does peace really look like?

Many people would define peace as the absence of conflict. In recent years God has used some powerful preaching to reveal to me that the closest thing I have to an idol – something that means more to me than it should – is that of a trouble-free life. Peace, in other words.

As is typical whenever we hold onto a notion that's not right, God challenged me several years ago about my notion of peace. This was a time when my whole life was submerged in total chaos and those around me were caught up in it and spreading it around. Life was far from trouble-free.

In the midst of that chaos I found myself praying for Paul's exhortation that he gave the church at Philippi. "And the peace of God, which transcends all understanding, will guard your hearts and your minds in Christ Jesus," Paul wrote in Philippians 4:7. I asked God to give me peace in the midst of all the chaos. I kept praying and the next time a situation became emotionally charged, God delivered. Before then I would have joined the escalating emotions and voices, but God filled me with a peace that "transcends all understanding" in that situation. I was amazed and gave God all the praise, because I knew this was not something I naturally had within me.

I still need to pray for continued peace, especially when chaos seems to reign. But now I have learned that peace is not the absence of conflict, but the very real presence of God in my life.

12   Sunshine Carrots

5 medium carrots, sliced and cooked in water until tender
1 tablespoon sugar
1 teaspoon cornstarch
¼ teaspoon salt
¼ teaspoon pepper
¼ teaspoon ground ginger
¼ cup orange juice
2 tablespoons butter

In saucepan, mix sugar, cornstarch, salt, pepper, and ginger. Add orange juice and cook until thick and bubbly. Stir in butter; toss with carrots.

Reading: Psalm 118:22-29

A former local radio personality had a unique gimmick. The talk radio station tuned to my car as I drive home to stay informed of traffic issues had a popular afternoon host who chatted about a variety of things in between the regular traffic and weather updates. At some point during his program, he generally asked for callers to give input or share stories related to the issue being discussed, which is pretty common radio talk show fare.

I noticed one day that most of the callers included a "Happy birthday, John!" in their greeting, which I thought was a nice acknowledgement of the host's special day. A couple of days later I heard callers doing the same thing. I found it a bit odd, but figured they were just off a few days on the actual date of the birthday, which is not so uncommon. As time wore on, however, I found that to be a regular practice of the callers. I considered that to be a gimmick of the host, for whatever reason. One time I heard a television meteorologist call to give a weather update and ask, "Did I hear right that today's your birthday?" The host chuckled and said, "No, it's a joke – I'll tell you about it sometime."

As I continued to hear callers regularly wish the host a happy birthday, I wondered what it would feel like to be constantly wished "happy birthday." For some it could be annoying. For others, however, it could be fun! Imagine what it would be like if every day was really your birthday, as you were treated specially and were immersed in festive and celebratory surroundings. I like the fresh, bright flavors of Sunshine Carrots – they're like a celebration for the taste buds! Yet they're simple enough to make any day of the week.

The psalmist recommends we revel on a daily basis. "This is the day the Lord has made; let us rejoice and be glad in it." (Psalm 118:24) That sounds like an invitation to celebrate every day as if it were your birthday! The verse basically reminds us that today is special because God made it. Cake and presents don't have to be part of our daily celebration, but being festive and rejoicing can. Celebrate today – just as if it were your birthday – every day!

13   Parmesan Potatoes

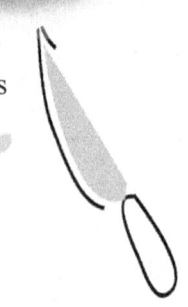

6 medium potatoes, peeled and cut into bite-sized chunks
¼ cup flour
¼ cup grated parmesan cheese
½ teaspoon salt
¼ teaspoon ground black pepper
6 tablespoons butter

Place butter in 9 x 13 baking dish while preheating oven to 375°. Meanwhile, combine flour, cheese, and seasonings in zipper-sealed bag; add potatoes and toss to coat. Placed coated potatoes in single layer of melted butter. Bake for 1 hour, stirring once.

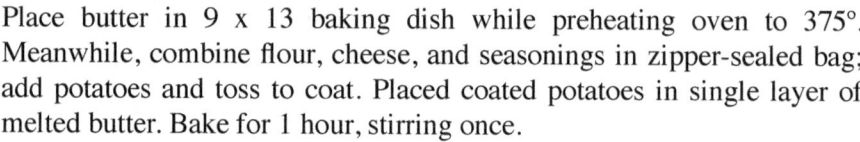

Reading: James 5:13-18

I remember a time when my son was having difficulty with something. He said he was praying about it, but I sensed he was missing the "powerful and effective" mark of a prayer that James talks about in that popular verse, 5:16.

I happened to be washing dishes when a thought occurred to me, so I called my son into the kitchen. I took a clear, plastic container and asked if it was clean. Of course it wasn't, so he said so. I dunked the container into the water and pulled it up again. "Is it clean now?" I asked. Again, it was still classified as dirty. I dipped the container into the water and took one swipe at it with my dish cloth before pulling it out again, asking the same question. It was improved, but my son acknowledged it was still dirty. At that point, the container re-entered the dish water and the dish cloth was applied heartily to the soiled areas. The container came up from the water once again. "How about now -- is it clean?" I asked. "Well, actually, you missed a little spot but it looks a lot better," was the reply.

The point I was trying to make was that a half-hearted prayer was not going to fix my son's problem any more than just dunking the dirty dish in the water was going to clean it. Correcting a wrong thought pattern or habit takes a lot of prayer, just like the container didn't get clean until I applied a lot of "elbow grease" to it. I've made Parmesan Potatoes countless times because they are very tasty, but many times the baking dish has required a little elbow grease to clean it thoroughly.

Before Jesus relays the parable of the persistent widow to His disciples, Luke tells us in 18:1 that the purpose was "to show them that they should always pray and not give up." In Ephesians 6:18, Paul reminds us, "And pray in the Spirit on all occasions with all kinds of prayers and requests. With this in mind, be alert and always keep on praying for all the Lord's people." Back in that passage in James, starting in verse 13, Jesus' brother spells out some reasons to pray: if you're in trouble, happy, sick, or have sinned. James even mentions in verses 17 and 18 that Elijah "prayed earnestly" that it wouldn't rain (and it didn't for 3 ½ years!) and then "again he prayed" so it would rain. That's what I call elbow grease!

All of this makes me ask, "How much elbow grease do I really put into my prayers?" We get requests via email, at church, in person -- how much effort do we put into those? I have to admit at times I do little more than dunk the request in a shallow stand of prayer. As I've prayed about this message, I have been convicted that these requests have come my way for a reason and deserve nothing less than concentrated elbow grease.

So... how much elbow grease do you put into your prayers? It's truly "powerful and effective" -- especially for the person saying the prayer.

Sunday Rice Casserole

1 cup long grain rice, uncooked
1/3 cup bell pepper, chopped
½ cup green onions and tops, chopped
2-ounce can mushroom stems and pieces, undrained
2 tablespoons vegetable or canola oil
1½ tablespoons Worcestershire sauce
Salt and pepper to taste
2 cups beef or chicken broth

Combine all ingredients in lightly-greased 2-quart casserole dish with tight-fitting lid. Bake, covered, at 350° for 45 minutes. Remove lid and toss rice before serving.

Reading: Ecclesiastes 5:1-7

Most of us have a routine established to get ready for church each week. We turn off the alarm, crawl out of bed and into the shower. Sometimes we begin preparing for the meal we'll eat after the service – maybe even prepping vegetables for some of the dishes, like this flavorful Sunday Rice Casserole. We get dressed in clothes we may have picked out the night before, finish our hygiene rituals and make sure our hair and accessories complete the look we want. Then we climb into the car and drive the same route to church that we took last week.

Sounds reasonable and fairly common. But did you ever think there may be more to getting ready for church?

"This is the church of the living God, which is the pillar and foundation of the truth" (1 Timothy 3:15b, NLT).

When I read that verse, I immediately considered that to be an appropriate prayer for my church. The first step in getting ready for church is making sure the church is ready for you – that it truly is a "pillar and foundation of the truth." If that doesn't describe your church, then there's something wrong that requires a change.

"Guard your steps when you go to the house of God. Go near to listen rather than to offer the sacrifice of fools, who do not know that they do wrong" (Ecclesiastes 5:1).

It occurred to me after I read the passage in 1 Timothy that it is equally important that I am ready for church, and the verse in Ecclesiastes is a good scripture prayer to accomplish that. I am to be mindful of why I'm going to church – it is to listen to God speaking, through the message, the music, and the members. I am to offer myself as a sacrifice for worship to the Lord. Those who attend church without the intent of worshipping the living God are giving a sacrifice of fools. They may fool others, but they don't fool God.

But the verse in Ecclesiastes also points out that some who "offer the sacrifice of fools" aren't aware that there's anything wrong with what they're doing. So I need to pray for those around me at church, that they, too, will "go near to listen".

Listening is very important, but having a heart ready to receive the word of God is also crucial. We are instructed in James 1:21 to "humbly accept the word planted in you."

Is your church ready for you? Are you ready for church?

Dressing/Stuffing

12 cups cubed bread
1 cup butter
¾ cup chopped onion
1 ½ cup chopped celery
1 teaspoon salt
1 teaspoon pepper
1 tablespoon poultry seasoning
1 can cream of celery soup

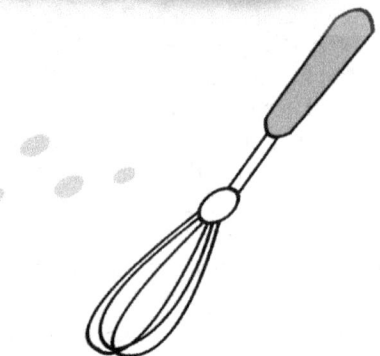

Melt butter in large skillet; add onion and cook over low heat until onion is browned. Add 3 cups of bread and toss until it begins to brown. Put rest of bread in large bowl and toss with browned cubes. Add remaining ingredients and toss to combine. Place in lightly-greased casserole dish, adding hot water or chicken broth if needed to moisten. Bake at 450° about 30 minutes or until done. If desired, this can also be used to stuff a 12-pound turkey.

Reading: Colossians 3:12-14

One thing I have looked forward to since I was a child preparing to observe a Thanksgiving feast was my mother's dressing. My mother is gone now, but I have the recipe. This is one great recipe -- so flavorful from the time you start sautéing the onions in the butter until it settles in your stomach next to that slice of turkey! This recipe is such a favorite of mine that I really have a difficult time enjoying any other dressing or stuffing (but that's <u>my</u> problem!).

Despite its magnificent flavor, this dressing recipe in its original form had a slight deficiency. Several years back I decided to talk to a "well-seasoned" cook about my little problem: it was crumbly. This recipe is made moist by adding water or broth, but it still likes to scatter its little bits of bread, onion and celery all over the dinner plate. The older cook's diagnosis: "You need a binder," she told me. She explained that the dish was crumbly because it didn't have an ingredient to hold everything together in one place. She said egg or cream-of-something soup would do the trick. It's the same principle as meatloaf, which would be little more than roasted, crumbled hamburger without an egg to hold it all together.

I appreciated the advice, but quite frankly was concerned that adding another ingredient would interfere with the delicate balance of robust flavors in the dish. Nevertheless, the next Thanksgiving I made my dressing with a binder (I don't even remember which I used -- the egg or soup). Lo, and behold, the dressing ingredients stuck to each other and the distinctive favor still shined through!

The Bible isn't silent about this issue either, because we would certainly fall apart and crumble if left to our own devices. The apostle Paul was a tentmaker but he might have had some culinary talents based on his words in Colossians 3:12-14: "Therefore, as God's chosen people, holy and dearly loved, clothe yourselves with compassion, kindness, humility, gentleness and patience. Bear with each other and forgive one another if any of you has a grievance against someone. Forgive as the Lord forgave you. And over all these virtues put on love, which binds them all together in perfect unity."

So it turns out this cook was very scriptural in her advice: "You need a binder!"

Creamy Pasta-Veggie Medley

2 ½ quarts water with 1 teaspoon salt
2 cups sun-dried tomatoes, sliced into thin strips
8 ounces rotini pasta
2 cups broccoli florets
1 large red bell pepper, chopped
3-4 green onions, chopped
15-ounce jar alfredo sauce
¼ cup fresh basil or parsley, chopped finely
Grated parmesan cheese

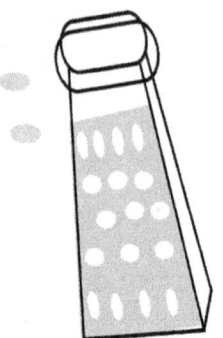

Bring water to boil in large pot over high heat while you wash, trim and prepare vegetables. When water reaches boiling point, transfer 1 ½ cups to small mixing bowl. Add sun-dried tomatoes and soak for 5 minutes; drain. Return water to rapid boil over high heat. Add pasta gradually, stirring to prevent sticking. Cook pasta for 3 minutes less than recommended. Add broccoli, peppers, and onions to pot; cook 3 minutes over high heat. Place glass measuring cup underneath a colander in the sink. Drain pasta and vegetables well in colander, then return immediately to pot. Stir in tomatoes, alfredo sauce, and herbs, adding reserved pasta liquid to achieve desired consistency. Serve topped with parmesan cheese.

Reading: Proverbs 18:21-24

I like how all the flavors in the Creamy Pasta-Veggie Medley complement each other, but I appreciate how well the light sauce holds everything together without being overly sticky. Sometimes we find ourselves in a sticky situation – and that can take any number of forms.

Some days it's worse than others. You know what I'm talking about. You try to make coffee in the morning and two filters stick together -- I mean, really stick! You know the drill: use your thumbs to try to locate some place where the two coffee filters aren't all but welded together, blowing as you go to encourage separation. You keep rotating the filters, around and around, waiting to catch your lucky break. One morning I may have broken a personal record on how long it took me to get the two filters separated.

When things like that stick together, it's frustrating! But it's not always a bad thing. Proverbs 18:24 reminds us: "One who has unreliable friends soon comes to ruin, but there is a friend who sticks closer than a brother." The Message uses this phrasing: "Friends come and friends go, but a true friend sticks by you like family." In his commentary on that verse, Matthew Henry writes, "In our troubles we expect comfort and relief from our relations, but sometimes *there is a friend*, that is nothing akin to us, the bonds of whose esteem and love prove stronger than those of nature, and, when it comes to the trial, will do more for us than a brother will."

I can personally attest to this, as I have a few very amazing, dear friends whose commitment and ability to stick with me through trials with unwavering support has given me untold amounts of strength and courage. I can never thank them enough, and have told them as much.

But Matthew Henry continues in his commentary: "Christ is a friend to all believers that *sticks closer than a brother*." There is no doubt of this in my mind or heart either. As much encouragement as my special friends have been for sticking together with me, nothing can compare to the friendship of Jesus! God's love mixed with our prayers creates a bond stronger than Super Glue, which makes sticking together an unspeakable joy!

Secret Sauce for Vegetables

The secret of this sauce is that it's so simple to make, yet no one will have a clue what's in it. It tastes like it took hours to prepare, and works well on both cooked and raw vegetables.

1 cup mayonnaise
1 ½ tablespoon soy sauce (or to taste)

Place mayonnaise in bowl and add desired amount of soy sauce. Mix well and serve.

From "How to Cook Like a Jewish Grandmother" by Marla Brooks; Pelican Publishing Company, Inc.; Copyright © 2005 By Marla Brooks. Used by permission.

Reading: Deuteronomy 29:26-29

The first Sunday of February 2014 marked two notable events which people attempted to predict the outcome in advance. Will Punxsutawney Phil see his shadow this Groundhog's Day? Will the Denver Broncos or the Seattle Seahawks win the Super Bowl? At that point, no one knew.

The late Christian author and speaker Barbara Johnson relates the story of a radio call-in show of which she was a participant. A woman called in with a long list of problems – including her house burning down – and wanted to know what she could do and where she could go. Barbara and the show's host were both bewildered at how to answer, until Barbara finally blurted out, "God only knows!"

I read a story once about a Polish rabbi who was walking in the city with his students one day. While they were on a hill, their attention was directed to the city below when they heard a great deal of noise. To their horror, they could see a group of rebels attacking the town. In despair, the rabbi lamented, "Oh, if only I were God!" The students were shocked by this statement and asked what the rabbi would do differently, to which the rabbi replied, in part, "If I were God, I would understand."

"The secret things belong to the Lord our God, but the things revealed belong to us and to our children forever, that we may follow all the words of this law" (Deuteronomy 29:29).

When I asked Marla Brooks, author of "How to Cook Like a Jewish Grandmother," for permission to use the recipe for secret sauce, she readily agreed. "I think it's too good not to share!" So much for secrets, but I totally agree with Marla – some things are just too good not to share! Learning the secret behind a great recipe is a bit of a thrill to me. I think that's because I gain a new level of understanding of what makes a recipe turn out so well.

We are not going to understand everything that happens on this earth. That's really hard for me – I feel like I can deal with situations better if a rational explanation is presented. But we must trust that there's a reason why God isn't revealing something to us. And in the end, it really doesn't matter if we understand, because oftentimes God is truly the only One who knows. The verse from Deuteronomy makes it clear that obedience is the not-so-secret ingredient that adds flavor to our lives.

Tamale Pie

1 pound lean ground beef
15-ounce can cream-style corn
15-ounce can diced tomatoes
1 teaspoon chili powder
½ teaspoon salt

½ cup chopped onion
½ cup chopped bell pepper
½ teaspoon garlic salt
¼ teaspoon black pepper
2/3 cup corn meal

Saute peppers and onion in oil in large skillet. When soft, add beef and cook until no longer pink. Add seasonings and stir to combine thoroughly. Add corn and tomatoes and heat until hot, then add corn meal and mix thoroughly. Pour into lightly-greased rectangular baking dish. Bake at 350° about 45 minutes or until brown.

Reading: Genesis 3:1-7

I tend to procrastinate when I need a new pair of glasses, telling myself that although I can't see perfectly, I can get by for just a little while longer with the pair I have. It has always amazed me how difficult it is to navigate once you get a new pair of glasses. You put the new and improved pair on, and when you try to walk the floor just seems so much different. Things just look, well, weird and almost out of proportion. With a new pair of glasses, you expect to be able to see clearly, without distortion.

It's easy for our vision to get distorted, as Eve discovered by the tree in the middle of the Garden of Eden. The first woman "saw that the fruit of the tree was good for food and pleasing to the eye ... [so] she took some and ate it" (Genesis 3:6). Eve knew she wasn't supposed to eat fruit from that particular tree, but it looked so good that she let the Devil talk her into eating it.

Professional chefs will tell you that you eat with your eyes first. Preparing the Tamale Pie recipe for the first time, I admit I was even more excited to taste it because it just looked colorful and inviting as all the ingredients came together. Maybe that's the anticipation Eve felt, so her vision became distorted.

Having distorted vision is one thing, but being blind is another. The Bible tells of a time when Jesus healed a man who was physically blind. Mark 8:25 says: "Once more Jesus put his hands on the man's eyes. Then his eyes were opened, his sight was restored, and he saw everything clearly." I am amazed at the concept that there was no period of adjustment -- the man immediately saw everything clearly!

Our Christian faith is like that, too. When we accept Jesus as our personal Lord and Savior, we look at things differently, and we are finally able to go the right direction. Psalm 16:11 is a praise to God for clarity of vision: "You have made known to me the path of life; you will fill me with joy in your presence, with eternal pleasures at your right hand." Daniel also praised God for giving him a clear vision in Chapter 2 and verse 23: "I thank and praise you, God of my ancestors: You have given me wisdom and power, you have made known to me what we asked of you, you have made known to us the dream of the king."

We are also promised that we can see EVERYTHING. Jesus promised His disciples in Luke 12:2: "There is nothing concealed that will not be disclosed, or hidden that will not be made known." As Christ's present-day disciples, we have that same promise. And Paul assures us in Romans 1:20 that God's presence is obvious: "For since the creation of the world God's invisible qualities — his eternal power and divine nature — have been clearly seen, being understood from what has been made, so that people are without excuse."

God longs to help us see clearly, and better vision is just a prayer away!

Ravioli Casserole

28-ounce jar spaghetti sauce
25-ounce package frozen ravioli, cooked and drained
16 ounces small-curd cottage cheese
16 ounces shredded mozzarella cheese
¼ cup grated parmesan cheese

Spread ½ cup sauce in lightly-greased 9 x 13 baking dish. Layer with half of the remaining ingredients (except parmesan); repeat layers. Sprinkle with parmesan cheese. Bake, uncovered, at 350° for 30-40 minutes or until bubbly. Let stand 5-10 minutes before serving.

Reading: 1 Kings 18:25-39

I was in the store one day when I noticed something unbelievable. I needed a box of bandages and was looking at two name-brand packages. The contents were the same – both contained 30 of the same size of flexible fabric bandages. And yet, one cost just 96 cents while the other cost $2.82! Now, the one that cost more was "the" name brand, but the other was also a well-known brand so that's the one I bought.

In comparison, the brand I bought is actually slightly shorter than the other brand. Since I mainly use them on my fingers to protect paper cuts or ailing hang nails, that is actually a bonus. Used in other places, the main thing is generally the size of the gauze pad that covers the boo-boo that's really important, and that area is the same. My husband commented he didn't think they're quite as good, but the price difference gave his vote to the cheaper brand. So I think I got a really good value on those bandages.

In this economy, people are looking for a good value. Ravioli Casserole is a good value on a couple of levels. The ingredients are readily available and reasonably priced. This is a large casserole so it will also feed a lot of people. This dish to me is like a "poor-man's lasagna," but the preparation and cooking times are significantly less than a traditional lasagna, yet to me it tastes as good. That's my idea of a good value!

I will admit I have some things that I am a "brand snob" about; some things are actually worth the extra money you pay for them because they taste or work better.

I didn't buy "the" brand of bandages, but I understand "the" God is the only way to go. Moses told Pharaoh in Exodus 8:10 that the whole purpose of the plague of frogs was so the ruler "may know there is no one like the Lord our God." In fact, when The Ten Commandments were handed down, sitting at the top at number one is "You shall have no other gods before me" (Exodus 20:2) – the Lord is "the" God!

It reminded me of the story in 1 Kings 18 when the prophet Elijah went head-to-head(s) with 450 prophets of Baal. The people agreed the prophets should build altars and sacrifice to their respective gods, asking the gods to set fire to the sacrifice. Elijah even let Baal's prophets go first. To make a long but interesting story short (check it out for yourself), Jehovah won. Verse 39 says: "When all the people saw this, they fell prostrate and cried, 'The Lord -- he is God! The Lord -- he is God!'"

In Psalm 77:13, Asaph reminds us of the good value we have in the Lord: "What god is as great as our God?" Accept no substitutes for "the" God.

Grilled Salsa Chops

Combine the following in a large zipper-seal bag:
1 ¼ cups Italian salad dressing
¾ cup salsa
1 tablespoon each: garlic powder, soy or teriyaki sauce, Worcestershire sauce, lemon juice, and dried basil leaves
½ tablespoon each garlic salt and hot sauce
1 t cayenne pepper

Add 6-10 pork loin chops (1/2" thick) to marinade. Refrigerate 4-6 hours, squeezing bag occasionally. Discard marinade and grill over medium coals 20-30 minutes or until done.

Reading: Psalm 119:97-104

One day I decided to come up with a marinade for grilled pork chops, and I was surprised at how well it consistently works! Italian salad dressing and salsa are combined with several other ingredients for a tasty marinade for pork loin chops. The marinade makes the meat come out juicy but also tasty because the flavors have had plenty of time to permeate the meat throughout.

That recipe that I've made for many years popped into my mind one Sunday morning when our pastor encouraged us in his sermon to "Read God's word and marinate in it." You can coat the outside of meat with sauce to give it a good flavor, but marinating it allows the flavors to become part of the protein and change it throughout – so much so that it's noticeable in every bite. In the same way, we can certainly learn truth from the Bible by reading it, but it can soak in deeper and become a part of our very being.

God advised Joshua to do just that as he was taking the reins of leading the Hebrew nation into the Promised Land. "Keep this Book of the Law always on your lips; meditate on it day and night, so that you may be careful to do everything written in it. Then you will be prosperous and successful" (Joshua 1:8).

The writer of Psalm 119 knew the value of meditating on God's word, as exhibited by these eight references to the practice. "I meditate on your precepts and consider your ways" (verse 15). "Though rulers sit together and slander me, your servant will meditate on your decrees" (verse 23). "Cause me to understand the way of your precepts; that I may meditate on your wonderful deeds" (verse 27). "I reach out for your commands, which I love, that I may meditate on your decrees" (verse 48). "May the arrogant be put to shame for wronging me without cause; but I will meditate on your precepts" (verse 78). "Oh, how I love your law! I meditate on it all day long" (verse 97). "I have more insight than all my teachers, for I meditate on your statutes" (verse 99). "My eyes stay open through the watches of the night, that I may meditate on your promises" (verse 148).

David advocated encouraging the younger generation to marinate in God's word as well, stating in Psalm 145:4-5: "One generation commends your works to another; they tell of your mighty acts. They speak of the glorious splendor of your majesty – and I will meditate on your wonderful works."

Submerse yourself in God's word. Let it slowly soak in and become a part of your inmost being. Marinate in it until the Lord's flavor has no choice but to come through!

President's Chicken

6-8 boneless, skinless chicken breasts
¼ cup butter or margarine
Juice of 1 lemon
½ teaspoon salt
½ teaspoon paprika
½ teaspoon dried, crushed basil leaves
½ teaspoon garlic powder
¼ teaspoon pepper

Preheat broiler to 425°. In small saucepan, mix together all ingredients except chicken. Cook over medium low heat until butter has melted. Place chicken breasts on broiler pan or foil-lined cookie sheet. Spoon half of sauce on chicken. Broil 20-30 minutes or until done, turning after 10 minutes and spooning remaining sauce on chicken.

Reading: 2 Corinthians 12:6-10

Sometimes it's best to just keep things simple. This chicken recipe is a long-time favorite of mine. It has a lot of good qualities that appeal to me – simple ingredients, simple preparation, and simply delicious! Good food doesn't have to be complicated, but sometimes we try to make it that way.

If you've never had the privilege of working with young children – preschool and elementary school age – you should really try it. The children are full of energy and usually very delightful, bringing a lot of joy to those around them.

Those who have taught this age group at church – whether in Sunday School, children's church, youth groups or Vacation Bible School – may have noticed something. Interaction is a must to keep their attention, so asking the children questions is a regular part of the lesson. Sometimes when it is a "who" question being asked, at least one child will answer "God" or "Jesus." There's at least one in every group. They must reason that they're in church, so "God" and "Jesus" can NEVER be the wrong answer!

As adults, we often miss that simplicity of believing that God is always the right answer. We come up with our own answers based on education and experience. And those answers – apart from God and His will – are many times the wrong ones.

Many people admire the apostle Paul because he got it right. Well-educated and well-spoken, Paul was stripped of everything to the point where he realized God was all he had – and, more importantly, all he needed.

Paul pointed this out to the church in Philippi, writing, "And my God will meet all your needs according to the riches of his glory in Christ Jesus" (Philippians 4:19). Talking about "the thorn in my flesh" while writing to the Corinthian church, Paul talked about being brought to reliance on God. He pens in 2 Corinthians 12: 8-9: "Three times I pleaded with the Lord to take it away from me. But he said to me, 'My grace is sufficient for you, for my power is made perfect in weakness'".

Paul knew it. Little kids know it. God is the answer. It's really just that simple!

Chicken 49'ers

4 or 5 boneless chicken breasts
8 ounces fresh mushrooms
1 large onion
1 green bell pepper
1 stick of butter
4 ounces Monterey Jack cheese, shredded

Melt half of butter in skillet. Chop mushrooms, onion, and green pepper and cook in butter. Remove and drain on paper towel. Cut chicken into bite-sized chunks and cook in remaining butter until done. Stir in vegetables; top with shredded cheese and let melt.

Reading: Jeremiah 33:1-9

Do you have a favorite Bible verse? When I came back to the church after being away for so long, people started asking me that question. I had never really thought about it, but since I was being asked, I figured it was something worth considering!

It was around that time that I heard Romans 8:31, which says at the end, "If God is for us, who can be against us?" Since I could easily identify with people being against me, it seemed like a good one to claim. I started telling people that was my favorite verse, and everyone agreed it was a nice one.

But then something happened.

I taught a lesson to children which said that Jeremiah 33:3 was "God's phone number," since the first few words are "Call to me and I will answer you." Then many years later, I read that verse again and read the rest of the verse: "... and tell you great and unsearchable things you do not know."

You have to understand that I'm not a person who is easily excitable, but when I think about this verse I get really excited! To think that God will not only answer what I ask of Him, but He wants to go beyond that! That God will share "great" things with me is, well, great, but what really gets me excited is that very last part: unsearchable things I don't know. It amazes me that the God of the universe wants to reveal to me things that are so awe-inspiring and beyond my scope of comprehension that I don't even know to ask about them! It reminds me how Paul in Ephesians 3:20 reminds us that God is "able to do immeasurably more than all we ask or imagine." It's all about God going above and beyond what our limited minds can even think about!

I still say "Wow!" when I think about Jeremiah 33:3!

I don't think anyone should feel they "have" to have a favorite verse. After all, there are so many great, inspiring words in the Bible it's difficult to choose just one. But if someone finds a verse they get excited about, they should latch onto it and see where God wants to take them with it.

I know of some people who say they have a "life verse" – basically a verse or passage from the Bible by which they try to live their lives. That's fine, but don't feel compelled to have a life verse, or that you have to stick with one verse as your favorite. Allow your favorite scripture selections to be as versatile an ingredient in your life as chicken is in cooking.

If you don't currently have a favorite verse, consider searching and the Lord will show you one that's a good fit for you based on where you are in life. He is still showing me more "unsearchable" things, and I can't wait for more!

Barry's Shrimp Creole

1/3 cup oil
1 pound medium shrimp
½ cup onion, minced
½ cup chopped bell pepper
1 cup water
2 bay leaves

¼ cup flour
1 clove garlic, minced
2 tablespoons parsley
8-ounce can tomato sauce
1 teaspoon salt
½ teaspoon cayenne pepper

Heat oil in large skillet or Dutch oven. Add flour and stir until light brown. Lower heat; add shrimp and cook about 3 minutes or until pink. Add garlic, onion, parsley, and bell pepper; cook 2 minutes. Raise heat; gradually add water, then remaining ingredients. Bring to a boil, then simmer, covered, for 20-30 minutes.

Reading: Ecclesiastes 9:10-12

Lying in his hospital bed, my father had the unique choice of determining when he wanted to die. The doctor told him that they would keep him on the life-giving oxygen until Dad decided he was ready to end his journey on earth. The doctor told my father and the family this on Friday afternoon, and Dad started talking about how he wanted to make it convenient for everyone. We surrounded Dad and told him not to worry about that, but instead to do what was best for him – he would be the only one to know when he was ready. Sunday morning he came to that conclusion.

Most of us don't get to pick when we leave this earth. Or how. Or where. "Moreover, no one knows when their hour will come. As fish are caught in a cruel net, or birds are taken in a snare, so people are trapped by evil times that fall unexpectedly upon them" (Ecclesiastes 9:12).

Because of this, it's important to be ready – whether we die in any number of ways or are taken up to Heaven when Christ comes again. Matthew 24:44 exhorts: "So you also must be ready, because the Son of Man will come at an hour when you do not expect him." Jesus talked more about being ready in Luke 12: 35-40:

"Be dressed ready for service and keep your lamps burning, like servants waiting for their master to return from a wedding banquet, so that when he comes and knocks they can immediately open the door for him. It will be good for those servants whose master finds them watching when he comes. Truly I tell you, he will dress himself to serve, will have them recline at the table and will come and wait on them. It will be good for those servants whose master finds them ready, even if he comes in the middle of the night or toward daybreak. But understand this: If the owner of the house had known at what hour the thief was coming, he would not have let his house be broken into. You also must be ready, because the Son of Man will come at an hour when you do not expect him."

Preparedness comes when we realize something is about to happen. Knowing my father's death was imminent, I had asked my friend Barry to preach the funeral a few months prior. When you take a trip, you pack clothes, make hotel arrangements, select sites to see, and plan activities to make the trip enjoyable. Have you packed your wardrobe of righteousness? Do you have the confirmation of your reservation in Heaven? Are you planning on walking the streets of gold or resting by the crystal sea after visiting the throne of the Almighty King? Will you spend your time talking with the saints or singing with the angels?

Are you ready?

Zippy Baked Fish

1 tablespoon Worcestershire sauce
1 ½ teaspoon lemon juice
½ pound fish filets
Salt and pepper to taste
¼ cup dry bread crumbs

Combine Worcestershire and juice. Dip serving-size pieces of fish in mixture, then season with salt and pepper. Dip in bread crumbs. Bake on lightly-greased foil-lined cookie sheet at 500° about 15 minutes. Serve with lemon wedges or tartar sauce. This will work well with any fish.

Reading: Luke 5:1-11

On a trip to my favorite lake spot, I found myself perched on the grass overlooking the spillway area. The sights and sounds of the spillway are breath-taking and also have a calming effect on me which was much needed that day.

While I was there, I noticed two young men fishing in the river at the base of the spillway. Personally, I don't go fishing, but I do like to eat fish, especially in tasty dishes like Zippy Baked Fish! I didn't notice if the two young men were having much luck, but after a time they left. As they left, I realized that their departure was not from a lack of fish in the river. Whatever their reason was for leaving at that time, it wasn't because there wasn't more fishing to do. Most people I know who enjoy fishing will usually say there will always be more fishing to do.

I find it fascinating that two occasions reported in the Bible are almost parallel. One passage is found in Luke 5:1-11 and is at the beginning of Jesus' ministry here on earth, while the other is recorded in John 21:1-6 after Christ's resurrection. In both cases, the fishermen – companions of Jesus – were out on the water and had not caught any fish all night long. But each time, Christ gave the command to put the nets down in the water. The fishermen obeyed and were rewarded with net-busting catches on both occasions.

Another interesting parallel is that each time, the fishermen didn't know who Jesus was. In Luke's passage, Jesus was just beginning His ministry and was starting to call disciples. But His authority must have been unquestionable, for in Luke 5 Peter calls Jesus "Master" and after mentioning the unproductive night he replies, "But because you say so, I will let down the nets" (verse 5). For the post-resurrection appearance, John records that "the disciples did not realize it was Jesus, (verse 4), yet they again obeyed when Christ directed, "Throw your net on the right side of the boat" (verse 6).

Back in Luke, we find great reassurance from the Lord as He told the fishermen that day, "Don't be afraid; from now on you will fish for people" (verse 10). Jesus knew there would always be more fishing to do.

Herbed Salmon & Asparagus

4 salmon filets
Salt & pepper to taste
1 pound asparagus, ends trimmed
1 lemon, thinly sliced (plus additional wedges for garnish)
½ cup butter, room temperature
1 tablespoon Italian seasoning
1 tablespoon minced garlic

Season salmon generously on both sides with salt and pepper. Lightly grease 4 pieces of foil, about 12 inches square. Place lemon slices on foil, top with salmon and asparagus. In small bowl, mix butter and seasonings. Divide evenly and drop dollops of herb butter on top of the salmon and asparagus. Fold foil tightly around each serving, being sure to seal the ends together tightly so the juices and butter don't run out while cooking. Grill over medium high heat for 6-8 minutes on each side, or bake at 400° for 20 minutes. Serve with lemon wedges.

Reading: Haggai 2:6-9

Abbott and Costello. Burns and Allen. Charlie Brown and Snoopy. Turkey and dressing. Ice cream and cake. Sour cream and chives. Some things just naturally go together – so much so that sometimes people can't imagine one thing without the other. Herbed salmon and asparagus have been added to my list!

The Lord promised yet another great pair during the rebuilding of the temple in Jerusalem. "'This Temple is going to end up far better than it started out, a glorious beginning but an even more glorious finish; a place in which I will hand out wholeness and holiness.' Decree of God-of-the-Angel-Armies" (Haggai 2:9, MSG). Wholeness and holiness from God – what a fantastic pairing! The apostle Paul apparently agreed. "May God Himself, the God who makes everything holy and whole, make you holy and whole, put you together – spirit, soul, and body – and keep you fit for the coming of our Master, Jesus Christ" (1 Thessalonians 5:23, MSG).

Holiness. We know the Lord is holy, so it makes sense that He can hand out that which He possesses. "'I am the Lord your God; consecrate yourselves and be holy, because I am holy,'" He commands the Hebrew nation in Leviticus 11:44. Paul mentions how it is God who "has saved us and called us to a holy life – not because of anything we have done but because of his own purpose and grace" (2 Timothy 1:9). Hebrews 12:14 offers this advice accompanied by an explanation: "Make every effort to live in peace with everyone and to be holy; without holiness no one will see the Lord."

Wholeness means we're complete, with nothing lacking. Paul reminds us in 1 Corinthians 1:7: "Therefore you do not lack any spiritual gift as you eagerly wait for our Lord Jesus Christ to be revealed." Peter adds in 2 Peter 1:3, "His divine power has given us everything we need for a godly life through our knowledge of him who called us by his own glory and goodness." It was God's glory and goodness that hung Jesus on the cross of Calvary for the sins of the world. "By that single offering, he did everything that needed to be done for everyone who takes part in the purifying process" (Hebrews 10:14, MSG).

Batman and Robin. Romeo and Juliet. Cheese and crackers. Peanut butter and jelly. Wholeness and holiness.

Sugar Cookies

1 cup butter or margarine
1 cup powdered sugar
1 cup vegetable oil
1 cup sugar
1 teaspoon vanilla extract
2 eggs
4 cups flour
1 teaspoon salt
1 teaspoon baking soda
1 teaspoon cream of tartar

Preheat oven to 350°.

Cream together the butter, oil and sugars. Add eggs and vanilla. Sift dry ingredients and add to butter mixture. Drop dough by teaspoons onto greased cookie sheets. Bake for 12 minutes or until golden brown. Makes approximately 6 dozen cookies.

Reading: 1 Corinthians 12:4-11

When I was a kid, we had an annual family reunion for my dad's side of the family. It was always held on the first Sunday in July, and always at someone's home. Like most family reunions, everyone was supposed to bring food to share. You never knew exactly what there would be to eat, but there were some "staples" that were just a given. Aunt Dot always made chicken and noodles and Aunt Lily made banana salad. Those two dishes were considered mandatory. A few times, Aunt Lily wasn't able to make it and you should have heard everyone complain about the missing banana salad!

I like to make a variety of things, but there are some things that I make that are frequently requested. This wonderful sugar cookie recipe was requested on a very regular basis by a former Sunday school class. If we were planning a class party, at least one person would hint, "Are you bringing sugar cookies?" For church funeral dinners, I am regularly asked to make a corn casserole as I've been told everyone enjoys it.

A friend had encouraged me to develop some new hobbies. I was unsure, saying I didn't have any talents other than a few he already knew about, like cooking and writing. "I bet you have talents you just don't know about," he replied. I was reluctant and voiced some concerns over some of the suggestions. But later I realized that if I'm so willing to try new recipes and share them with others, why don't I have the same attitude about talents?

The New Testament talks a lot about spiritual gifts and talents, with the biggest sections coming in Romans 12 and 1 Corinthians 12. Gifts such as teaching, serving, giving, prophesying, wisdom, knowledge, faith, encouragement and showing mercy are listed. The passages make it clear that all gifts are important and we are not all given the same gifts, but they also caution against limiting ourselves. "Eagerly desire the greater gifts," Paul writes in 1 Corinthians 12:31, and then in 1 Corinthians 14:12 he encourages, "Since you are eager to have spiritual gifts, try to excel in gifts that build up the church."

What do you bring to the table? There's nothing wrong with the old stand-bys, but why not broaden yourself and open up to see what talents you may have hidden? Ask God to show you what lies underneath so you can uncover those talents to be used in greater service to Him. As believers embark on new adventures in search of ways to serve, the feast will be bountiful as we each bring more to the table!

Persimmon Cookies

1 cup + 2 tablespoons sugar
½ cup butter
1 egg, lightly beaten
1 cup persimmon pulp, with 1 teaspoon baking soda
½ cup applesauce
1 teaspoon orange peel
½ teaspoon nutmeg
½ teaspoon ground cloves
½ teaspoon ground cinnamon
Pinch of salt
2 cups flour
1 cup nuts
1 cup raisins

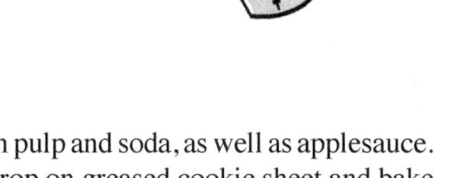

Cream sugar and butter. Add egg, then pulp and soda, as well as applesauce. Add spices, flour, nuts and raisins. Drop on greased cookie sheet and bake at 350° for 10-15 minutes.

Reading: Isaiah 49:13-18

My father loved making these persimmon cookies for the holidays. I'm not sure where the family acquired the recipe, but we've had it a long time. Dad, however, liked to try different flavors and change things up a bit, whether it was the type of nut, seasoning, or any other element with which he chose to experiment.

The cookie has a consistency of cake with several spices, so most people enjoyed them even if they had no idea that persimmons are usually very tart on their own. My husband was compelled to try them after we were married, and thought they were pretty good – except the fact that he's not a fan of raisins. He shared that comment, and the next batch sent to us had dried cranberries in them. My husband seemed surprised that Dad would switch out the raisins in favor of cranberries.

I wasn't the least bit surprised. One thing my father taught me by example was that remembering details are important when you love someone. Dad showed his love for my husband by swapping out the raisins for dried cranberries for a special, tasty batch of persimmon cookies.

Our Heavenly Father also knows the importance of details for those He loves. "Even the very hairs of your head are all numbered," Jesus told the Twelve Disciples in Matthew 10:30.

I am overwhelmed about how important I am to God, and how He poetically shares that truth with me in Isaiah 49:15-16a: "Can a mother forget the baby at her breast and have no compassion on the child she has borne? Though she may forget, I will not forget you! See, I have engraved you on the palms of my hands."

Let those words soak into your soul: "I will not forget you ... I have engraved you on the palms of my hands." Such love!

And that level of love breeds intimacy that allows us to share our innermost needs with God. "Cast all your anxiety on him because he cares for you," we're told in 1 Peter 5:7.

The apostle Paul assures us in 1 Corinthians 8:3, "But whoever loves God is known by God." God knows we get scared. He knows our strengths and weaknesses. He knows what we need even before we ask (Matthew 6:8).

This same God who knows all these important details about us also knows the trivial things, like the number of hairs we have.

And when we prefer cookies with no raisins.

Creamy Pudding Dessert

8-ounce package cream cheese, softened
2 ½ cups milk, divided
2 packages instant vanilla or French vanilla pudding (4-serving size)
24 cream-filled chocolate sandwich cookies, crushed

Beat cream cheese until very soft. Gradually add ½ cup milk and blend until smooth. Add remaining milk and instant pudding; mix. Beat at lowest speed of electric mixer until blended, about 1 minute. Stir in crushed cookies. Chill at least 2 hours.

Reading: 2 Corinthians 4:16-18

I used to work at a place that held a monthly food day to celebrate birthdays among the office workers. Everyone would bring food to be enjoyed throughout the day and I made this dessert on one such occasion. With the chocolate sandwich cookies providing the appropriate visual effect, I labeled it "Older Than Dirt Pudding!" It seemed fitting to me because one of the guys was having a milestone birthday and it was pretty common – even expected – that some of the festivities included a certain degree of orneriness!

Food typically plays a key role in celebrations, but so do presents. No matter how much loot you rake in on a birthday, Christmas or anniversary, you just can't beat what God gives us every day of the year. With all the blessings He gives us, ageless wisdom is one I especially appreciate.

There are so many examples of God's ageless wisdom in His Word -- which some consider outdated -- that I could write pages! But I have my own favorite example, and it's found in 2 Corinthians 4.

For those of you who haven't rushed to grab your Bible yet, let me tell you that this chapter sometimes has a title like "Treasures in Jars of Clay" in many editions. The chapter talks about mercy first of all; then touches on such things as knowledge and God's glory. Verse 7 tells us, "But we have this treasure in jars of clay to show that this all-surpassing power is from God and not from us." Wisdom tip #1: Any wisdom you have didn't come from yourself. How humbling, and yet very appropriate.

But I really love how the chapter ends, as verses 16-18 speak volumes about ageless wisdom. "Therefore we do not lose heart. Though outwardly we are wasting away, yet inwardly we are being renewed day by day. For our light and momentary troubles are achieving for us an eternal glory that far outweighs them all. So we fix our eyes not on what is seen, but what is unseen, since what is seen is temporary but what is unseen is eternal."

Wisdom tip #2: Don't lose heart. Wisdom tip #3: God will renew us day by day. Wisdom tip #4: Troubles are light and momentary (no matter how they may feel at the time). Wisdom tip #5: Eternal glory outweighs troubles. Wisdom tip #6: Shift our focus from earthly trials to heavenly glories. That's certainly a lot of ageless wisdom packed into three verses!

Younger people may not be able to identify with that "outwardly we are wasting away" line, but the rest of those verses certainly speak volumes of wisdom to everyone of all ages. Since God himself is ageless, it just stands to reason that His wisdom would be nothing less!

Apple Pie

5-6 medium apples, cored, peeled and sliced thin
1 ½ tablespoons lemon juice   ½ cup sugar
2 tablespoons flour   1 teaspoon grated lemon peel
½ teaspoon ginger   ½ teaspoon cinnamon
2 tablespoons butter, cut into 6 pieces

Toss apple slices with lemon juice. Mix together sugar, flour, lemon peel, ginger, and cinnamon; stir into apples. Spoon into unbaked easy pie crust (below). Top with butter pieces. Add top crust; seal edges and cut slits near center. Bake in 400° oven for 45-55 minutes or until crust is golden brown (after about 35 minutes or so you'll probably need to cover edge of crust with foil). Remove from oven and cool on rack.

Easy Pie Crust:
Whisk together:
2/3 cup vegetable oil
2/3 cup milk

Stir into 2 cups flour. Makes 2 pie crusts.

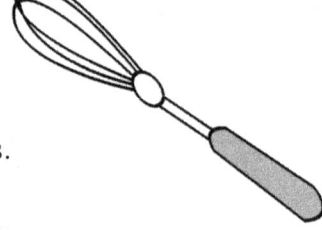

Reading: Jeremiah 6:10-19

I was taking a walk one day when I came to a fork in the road – literally. There was a shallow pothole at an intersection I cross and there was a dinner fork inside that pothole! Being easily amused, I found the whole scenario interesting. I thought about picking up the fork in the road, but decided against it. The pothole was pretty small so I don't think it was much of a road hazard, plus I wanted others to be amused along with me.

The next day on my walk, the fork was no longer "in" the road but had landed on top of the pavement. It was at that point I decided to take the fork in the road. It had apparently been run over repeatedly because it is quite scratched up and any previous hint of curves is now missing (which gives new meaning to the term "flatware"!). I would never eat apple pie – or anything else – with the fork, but I washed and kept it as a reminder of my decision to "take the fork in the road."

During our walk of faith, we often encounter proverbial forks in the road. I know I sometimes try to convince myself to take the path I want and then will later use the excuse that the wrong path didn't look wrong because, like my flattened and battered dinner fork, the shape of the path was somewhat distorted.

God has a different view of these forks in the roads, sometimes known as crossroads. He spells it out very clearly in Jeremiah 6: 16: "This is what the Lord says: 'Stand at the crossroads and look; ask for the ancient paths, ask where the good way is, and walk in it, and you will find rest for your souls." The unfortunate part is the last sentence of that verse where Jeremiah records the response of the Israelites: "But you said, 'We will not walk in it'." It doesn't get any better in the next verse, when God says he put watchmen over them and advised them to listen to the sound of the trumpet, but the people refused to listen. Pending destruction was promised as the punishment for their disobedience.

When you reach a fork in the road or a crossroads, the first thing you need to do is ask for directions. We need to "ask where the good way is and walk in it," otherwise we run the risk of getting lost and facing destruction. Obedience, on the other hand, is always rewarded with something good at the end of the fork!

Paradise Pumpkin Pie

8-ounce package cream cheese
1/2 teaspoon vanilla
1 unbaked deep-dish 9-inch pie shell
1 1/4 cup canned pumpkin
2 beaten eggs
1/4 cup white sugar
1/4 teaspoon salt
3/4 cup chopped pecans
3 tablespoons each: butter, softened; flour; & brown sugar

1/4 cup white sugar
1 egg, slightly beaten
1 cup evaporated milk
1/4 cup brown sugar
1 teaspoon cinnamon
1/4 teaspoon ground nutmeg

In small mixer bowl, beat together cream cheese, 1/4 cup white sugar, vanilla and 1 egg until smooth. Chill for at least 30 minutes. Turn into pie shell. Combine pumpkin, milk, 2 eggs, sugars and seasonings. Carefully ladle over cream cheese mixture. Cover edge of pie with foil. Bake in 350° oven for 25 minutes. Remove foil; bake 25 minutes more. Meanwhile, combine the pecans, butter, flour and brown sugar with fork. Sprinkle over pie. Bake for 10-15 minutes until a knife inserted near the center comes out clean. Cool on wire rack. Keep refrigerated.

Reading: Revelation 21:1-5

My husband and I decided to break up the Midwest winter with a week-long trip to Florida. After checking in, the bell hop took us to our room and talked about various amenities of the property. He left us with these words: "Welcome to Paradise!"

A case could be made that we were in Paradise. It was 10 degrees when we boarded the plane, and in the 60s when we landed in Florida. Sunshine. Palm trees. White beach. Cabanas. But it really wasn't Paradise: Out-of-date room décor, mold on the foundation of the bed, a very weak shower head, cold Gulf water and breezes. Plus, we had to pay for everything!

No, Florida isn't Paradise, even in the winter to a Midwesterner. My reservation to Paradise has actually been booked, although it has nothing to do with a decadent, flavor-packed pie.

As Jesus hung on the cross dying, one of the criminals also being crucified recognized Him as the promised Messiah: "… 'Jesus, remember me when you come into your kingdom.' Jesus answered him, 'Truly I tell you, today you will be with me in paradise'" (Luke 23:42-43).

Revelation 21 and 22 give some snapshots of the features we'll find in Paradise: Walls of jasper, a city of gold so pure it's clear, precious stones in the foundation, gates of pearl, and more. At the center of it all are the thrones of God and the Lamb, Jesus. "And I heard a loud voice from the throne saying, 'Look! God's dwelling place is now among the people, and God himself will be with them, and he will dwell with them. They will be his people, and God himself will be with them and be their God. He will wipe every tear from their eyes. There will be no more death or mourning or crying or pain, for the old order of things has passed away'" (Revelation 21:3-4).

Sounds wonderful, doesn't it? But Paradise won't be as crowded as we think. "Not everyone who says to me, 'Lord, Lord' will enter the kingdom of heaven, but only the one who does the will of my Father who is in heaven" (Matthew 7:21). Jesus explained what it will be like for those who don't go to Paradise. "This is how it will be at the end of the age. The angels will come and separate the wicked from the righteous and throw them into the blasting furnace, where there will be weeping and gnashing of teeth" (Matthew 13:49-50.)

Paradise is definitely the more desirable destination, so make every effort to bring your family and friends on this eternal trip. Then look forward to the day when Jesus says, "Welcome to Paradise!"

Fudge Brownie Pie

1 cup sugar
2 eggs
1/3 cup unsweetened baking cocoa
1/4 teaspoon salt
1/2 cup chopped pecans, optional
1/2 cup butter or margarine, melted
1/2 cup all-purpose flour
1 teaspoon vanilla extract
Optional: Whipped cream or ice cream; strawberries, optional

In a mixing bowl, beat sugar and butter. Add eggs; mix well. Add flour, cocoa and salt. Stir in vanilla and (optional) nuts. Pour into a greased 9-in. pie pan. Bake at 350° for 25-30 minutes or until almost set. Serve with whipped cream or ice cream and strawberries if desired.

Reading: 1 Corinthians 15:46-58

Driving down the highway I noticed a very large motor home, and the words "Someday Came" on the back. You can just imagine it: for years as they toiled hard at their jobs and at home, the couple would sigh in the midst of their exhaustion and say, "someday we won't have to work so hard. We'll buy a big motor home and travel." And so it happened: someday came. And they want others to know about it!

It's the hope of many – "someday" things will be better than they are now. It's the dream that keeps them going through the hard times. The great news is that for those who believe in God, "someday" is more than just a dreamy hope. For me, my "someday" includes being able to eat things like Fudge Brownie Pie (my favorite dessert) guilt free!

In Psalm 10:14, we read a comment addressed to the Lord: "But you know all about it – the contempt, the abuse. I dare to believe that the luckless will get lucky someday in you. You won't let them down: orphans won't be orphans forever" (MSG).

The prophet Jeremiah gave the Israelites in captivity hope for the future as he delivered a message from God: "Yes, fields will once again be bought and sold – deeds signed and sealed and witnessed ... For someday I will restore prosperity to them. I, the Lord, have spoken!" (Jeremiah 32:44, NLT).

God Himself offers words of confidence in the future, as recorded in Hosea 11:10: "For someday the people will follow me. I, the Lord, will roar like a lion. And when I roar, my people will return trembling from the west." (NLT) Jesus told His disciples, "You don't understand now what I am doing, but someday you will" (John 13:7, NLT).

The New Testament is loaded with promises of much better things to come "someday" for those who believe in Christ:

"'Men of Galilee,' they said, 'why are you standing here staring into heaven? Jesus has been taken from you into heaven, but someday he will return from heaven in the same way you saw him go!'" (Acts 1:11, NLT).

"Just as we are now like the earthly man, we will someday be like the heavenly man." (1 Corinthians 15:49, NLT)

"In the same way, the good deeds of some people are obvious. And the good deeds done in secret will someday come to light" (1 Timothy 5:25, NLT).

For the owners of the motor home, "Someday Came." For believers in Christ, "Someday WILL Come." And that is really something others ought to know about!

AUTHOR'S NOTES

As much as I enjoy cooking and writing devotions, I love helping people develop a regular, personal time with the Lord, which I call a "quiet time." My faith journey and spiritual growth have been greatly enhanced by this practice, which I mentioned in the reflection with the recipe for Granola Bars. Although I would frequently try to start my day by reading the Bible, it wasn't until I discovered how to do that in a meaningful way that involved applying and responding to the Scripture reading that I felt like I got my faith footing.

God is always there for us, but it's up to us to develop those spiritual habits to create a fertile soil for the seeds He wants to plant in us. I believe that the admonition Joshua gave to the Hebrew people just before entering the Promised Land applies to us: "Consecrate yourselves, for tomorrow the Lord will do amazing things among you." (Joshua 3:5) Basically, we need to make holy preparations to let God do the amazing things He plans to do in our lives. Attending church and praying are beneficial, but the way we are able to personally connect with God during a regular quiet time rooted in the Bible is how we consecrate ourselves.

Honestly, the opportunity to do this is extremely meaningful to me. So while I invite you to follow me on my Facebook page, Reflections & Recipes, I also strongly encourage you to contact me at LivingDevo@outlook.com. I'd be happy to answer any questions, or even mentor you toward developing a regular quiet time. I'm convinced that once the habit takes hold, it will strengthen your faith and change your life for the better as it has mine!

ACKNOWLEDGEMENTS

As I have been working on *Strength for the Body & Soul*, it occurred to me that I'm surrounded by PETS, and none of them have fur or feathers! These are Patient, Encouraging, and Talented Souls that have greatly blessed me through the process. Of course, at the top of the list is my husband Dave, who has learned that I can be very determined once I get an inspiration for a project! My creative team of Vicky Pannella and Anita Leppert have been so invaluable in a myriad of ways. I can't imagine having done this project without the advice and assistance of these two wonderful, incredibly creative and talented ladies, who I'm also proud to call my friends.

There are other friends who have supported and encouraged me in other ways – sometimes just simply being available to bounce ideas off of or listen to me talk about the book when I just needed to talk about it. Valerie Gaddis and Rex Brown are my siblings in Christ, and for many years have enriched my life by being a part of it. They are absolutely the best friends I've ever had and I couldn't cherish them more. My prayer partner Sharron Sedziol and another dear friend, Bob Mulvaine, also supported me in a variety of ways, particularly with their prayers and friendship when I would get discouraged and doubt myself, or just need an emotional lift. Over the years, many others have inspired and encouraged me in my devotion-writing endeavors, and each one has meant so much to me.

But above all, it is the mercy of my Heavenly Father, the unconditional love of my Lord and Savior Jesus Christ, and the gentle guidance of the Holy Spirit that have sustained me in all situations. God has truly blessed me, and strengthened my body and soul!

"Look to the Lord and His strength;
seek His face always."
Psalm 105:4

www.ingramcontent.com/pod-product-compliance
Lightning Source LLC
Chambersburg PA
CBHW062146100526
44589CB00014B/1699